Marco M

He's a joker who loves
messing abo...
always mear...
if he sometimes gets
things wrong.

Philippa Feltpen

A real peacemaker, she
helps keep the other
Pens in order by sorting
out arguments and giving
good advice.

Waxy Max

He's very sporty and
football mad. On the
outside, he's tough,
but underneath he's
got the biggest heart.

I think this one's
going to be a good
one! Let's see …

Squiggle and Splodge

The Scribble twins! They're
both quiet, both shy.
Although they may not
look alike, they do almost
everything together.

Enter …

Urrrr, let's have a look inside ...

'Faith' – what's that about?

Pens

Helping you to get to know God more

Trusting God

Written by
Alexa Tewkesbury

Every day a short Bible reading is brought to life with the help of the Pens characters. A related question and prayer apply this to daily life. Written in four sections, two focusing on the lives of Pens and two on Bible characters, young children will be inspired to learn more of God and His Word.

What's inside?

Faith in our Father

Day 1

Faith and the Friends – Jesus the healer

Day 10

God of Grace

Day 16

Jonah's Journey – Enough grace for everyone

Day 25

Mixed Sources
Product group from well-managed
forests and other controlled sources
www.fsc.org   Cert no. SGS-COC-003963
© 1996 Forest Stewardship Council

'We know that in all things God works for good with those who love him …' (Romans 8 v 28)

Philippa's promise

Pens were off to the cinema.

'We need to leave now,' worried Gloria, 'otherwise we might be late.'

But there was no sign of Philippa.

'I'll wait for her,' said Marco.

'You'll miss the film,' chivvied Gloria.

'No, I won't,' he replied. 'Philippa's promised to be here in time, and she will be.'

Pens set off and Marco waited. Not for long, though. Philippa arrived with time to spare.

'Thanks for waiting for me,' she smiled.

'That's all right,' grinned Marco. 'I knew you'd be here because you promised.'

God has made promises to us and we can trust Him to keep them.

Where can we find out about God's promises?

Pens Prayer
Lord God, thank You so much that You've promised to be with me always. Please teach me to trust in You. Amen.

5

Day 2 — Faith in our Father

'… build up your strength in union with the Lord and by means of his mighty power.' (Ephesians 6 v 10)

Tea for Pens

If only …

… if *only* I was BRAVE

6

Squiggle raised an eyebrow. 'Why do you want to be brave?'

'I want to invite Pens to tea,' Splodge answered, 'but I'm worried they won't want to come.'

'Only one way to find out,' said Squiggle. 'Let's ask them.'

'Oh no, I'm a bit too scared to ask them,' murmured Splodge.

'Charlotte says that God helps us to be brave. Let's go and ask them together,' encouraged Squiggle.

So off they went to ask every single Pen to tea …

And every single Pen said – 'YES!'

Squiggle and Splodge live here

When we put our faith in God, He will help us to do even the things we find difficult.

Do you need to ask God to help you today?

Pens Prayer

Dear Father God, if I ever feel scared or worried, I want to remember that You will always help me when I ask You to. Amen.

7

Faith in our Father

'The LORD protects me from all danger; I will never be afraid.' (Psalm 27 v 1)

A **big** decision

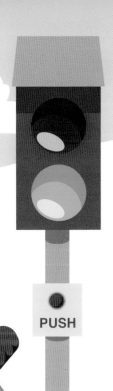

Splodge wanted to learn to cross the road by herself.

'Who can I ask to help me?' she wondered.

She thought of Max, but – 'No,' she decided. 'Not Max.'

She thought of Gloria, but – 'No,' she decided. 'Not Gloria.'

She thought of Denzil, but – 'No,' she decided. 'Not Denzil.'

'Who's going to help you, Splodge?' asked Charlotte.

'I don't know,' shrugged Splodge. 'I'm just not sure who to ask.'

'We all love you and will always try to help you,' said Charlotte. 'We'd be sad if we thought you didn't trust us.'

It makes God happy when we put our faith and trust in Him to take care of us.

How can you show God that you trust Him?

Pens Prayer

Lord God, thank You so much for looking after me today. Amen.

9

'… in all things you are faithful, O LORD.' (Psalm 89 v 8)

Philippa's faith

Marco was trying to teach himself to skip with a skipping rope.

It's very good exercise. It'll help to keep you healthy.

'I can't do it,' said Marco crossly. 'I've tried and I've tried, and I just CAN'T DO IT!'

'Ask God to help you,' suggested Philippa. 'That's what I do when I find something hard.'

'But this is just skipping,' said Marco. 'Why would God want to help me with *just skipping*?'

'God wants us to trust Him for everything,' smiled Philippa. 'If it matters to you, it matters to God.'

 God wants us to have faith that He'll be with us in all the things we do.

Apart from having exercise, how else can you keep yourself strong and healthy?

Pens Prayer

In the big things and in the little things, Lord God, thank You so much for being right beside me. Amen.

Faith in our Father

'… I, the LORD your God, am with you wherever you go.'
(Joshua 1 v 9)

Sad
Charlotte

Charlotte was sad. She didn't know why.

She didn't feel like smiling.

She didn't feel like chatting.

She didn't even feel like singing – and *that* was making her sadder still.

'I'm just not myself today,' she sighed. 'Pens are used to a cheerful Charlotte. They won't want to be my friends if I'm feeling like this.'

'That's not right,' said Max. 'We all have sad days. We can't help it. But it doesn't change how we feel about each other. Pens will be friends no matter what. Always.'

 With faith, we can trust in God to be with us whether we're feeling happy or sad.

How could you show God's love to someone who is sad?

Pens Prayer

Thank You, my loving God, that You are my Friend whatever the day brings. Amen.

13

Faith in our Father

'Everything is possible for the person who has faith.'
(Mark 9 v 23)

Squiggle learns to skate

14

Squiggle loved watching people roller-skate.

She enjoyed the speedy way skaters zipped along. She shrieked if skaters did clever tricks like skating on one leg or jumping in the air. She laughed at the way the wind whooshed through skaters' hair as they whizzed past.

But Squiggle wouldn't skate herself. She was too scared.

'I'll help you,' said Gloria. 'I can hold you up so you don't fall.'

Squiggle wasn't sure. 'What happens if you let me go?'

'But I won't let you go,' said Gloria.

And Gloria didn't. Soon, Squiggle was skating all by herself.

 When we have faith in God to take care of us, He will never let us down.

What are you learning to do at the moment?

Pens Prayer

Father God, I really praise You that I can depend on You COMPLETELY. Amen.

Day 7 — Faith in our Father

'To have faith is to be … certain of the things we cannot see.' (Hebrews 11 v 1)

Where's the wind?

It was very windy.

Shall we take your new kite outside?

Denzil wasn't sure. 'I suppose we could … but supposing it doesn't fly?'

'It'll fly,' laughed Philippa. 'Look at the wind!'

'That's the trouble,' frowned Denzil. 'I can't *see* the wind.'

'But you can see what it does,' said Philippa. The trees swayed.

'You can feel it move,' said Philippa. Cold air blew in their faces.

'You can hear it coming,' said Philippa. The wind whistled past.

'No, you can't *see* the wind,' she added, 'but you know that it's blowing.'

We cannot see God but, with faith, we can find Him in the beauty of the world He has made for us.

What kind of boat needs the wind to make it move?

Pens Prayer

Dear Lord God, please give me the faith to trust that You are always with me, watching over me. Amen.

Day 8 — Faith in our Father

'... your light must shine before people, so that they will see the good things you do and praise your Father in heaven.' (Matthew 5 v 16)

Ready to help

18

Squiggle and Splodge had bad colds so Pens were helping out.

Gloria and Marco helped with the shopping.

Denzil and Philippa helped with the cleaning.

Max and Charlotte helped with the washing.

Sharpy helped make Squiggle and Splodge laugh by dashing round in circles trying to catch his tail.

'Why are you all being so kind?' asked Squiggle.

'It makes God happy,' replied Charlotte. 'Helping out is a way of showing His love.'

'In that case,' smiled Splodge, 'God must have REALLY BIG LOVE for us.'

If others see God in the kind things we do, they might find it easier to put their faith in Him.

What could you do to help at home this week?

Pens Prayer

Please let Your love shine through me, Lord God. I want others to know You because they know me. Amen.

19

'I place myself in your care … you are a faithful God.'
(Psalm 31 v 5)

The bad ankle

I'm SO bored.

Max had hurt his ankle playing football and wasn't allowed to run around outside until it was better.

'It's not fair,' he grunted. 'When can I go out again?'

'When your ankle's all right,' said Denzil. 'Too soon – and you'll make it worse.'

'Exactly,' agreed Charlotte, 'and if you make it worse, you'll have to stay indoors even longer.'

Max still wasn't happy, but he knew his friends were right. He nodded his head and didn't argue. After all, they only wanted him to get better.

We can have faith in God that He only wants what's best for us.

If you ever hurt yourself, who looks after you?

Pens Prayer

Dear Lord, each new day, help me to trust You and follow You. Amen.

FAITH AND THE FRIENDS
Jesus the healer

Day 10

'The power of the Lord was present for Jesus to heal the sick.' (Luke 5 v 17)

The
full
house

One day, Jesus was sitting in a house teaching people about God. Everyone loved to hear Him talking. He could also make people better if they were ill. So Jesus was rather popular.

But the house Jesus was visiting wasn't very big, and such a huge crowd had come to listen that it was absolutely full. There wasn't room for one person more. Not even someone very small.

Jesus used the power God had given Him to help people, and to show them God had sent Him.

How can you spend time with Jesus?

Pens Prayer

Lord Jesus, help me remember to spend time with You because I know You always want to spend time with me. Amen.

Day 11

'Some men came carrying a paralysed man on a bed, and they tried to take him into the house and put him in front of Jesus.' (Luke 5 v 18)

No Way in

While Jesus was busy inside the house, some men arrived with their sick friend. The poor man was so ill he couldn't move. He could only lie on a little bed while his friends carried him.

The sick man's friends wanted him to meet Jesus but, because of the crowds, they couldn't even get near the front door. They looked at each other and frowned. They knew Jesus would help. They knew Jesus could make their friend well.

What they didn't know was how to get into the house.

The men had faith that Jesus would make their sick friend better.

Who do you trust to teach you and take care of you? Say thank you to God for them.

Pens Prayer

Teach me, Lord Jesus, to put my trust in You every day. Amen.

Faith and the Friends
Jesus the healer

Day 12

'So they carried him up on the roof ...'
(Luke 5 v 19)

A good idea

One of the sick man's friends had an idea.

'All the people trying to get close to Jesus are on the ground,' he said. 'Let's climb up to the roof. We might find a way into the house through there.'

So up they all went, carrying their sick friend on his bed. It was very difficult, but once on the roof, they began to make a hole; a hole just large enough to lower their friend through ... down, down – and right in front of Jesus.

Nothing could stop the sick man's friends from getting him in to see Jesus.

If someone in your family isn't feeling well, how can you help to look after them?

Pens Prayer

Dear Jesus, thank You that You do wonderful things when we have faith in You. Amen.

Faith and the Friends
Jesus the healer

Day 13

'When Jesus saw how much faith they had, he said to the man, "Your sins are forgiven, my friend."' (Luke 5 v 20)

Amazing faith

The people in the house were surprised to see a bed dropping slowly down towards them. They were even more surprised to see the poor man who was lying on it.

But Jesus just smiled.

First, He smiled up at the men on the roof. 'What amazing faith you have,' He said.

Next, He smiled down at their friend on the bed. 'Everything's all right,' He said. 'The bad things you've done are forgiven.'

When we put our faith in Jesus, it makes Him very happy.

How can you get to know Jesus better?

Pens Prayer

Lord Jesus, please help me to trust that You will always take care of me. Amen.

'God is the only one who can forgive sins!'
(Luke 5 v 21)

Jesus ASKS a question

Some other teachers were in the house. When they heard Jesus forgive the sick man for everything he'd done wrong, they were angry.

'How can you say that?' they snapped. 'Only God is able to forgive sins.'

Once more, Jesus smiled. 'This poor man can't even move,' He said, 'so what is easier to do? To forgive the bad things in his life or to tell him to get up and walk?'

No one knew what to say. They just watched and waited.

Jesus knew His Father God was with Him in everything He did.

If you are ever sad or worried about something, do you talk to Jesus about it?

Pens Prayer

Thank You, Jesus, that I can trust in You completely. Amen.

Faith and the Friends
Jesus the healer

Day 15

'I tell you, get up, pick up your bed, and go home!'
(Luke 5 v 24)

Jesus heals

Jesus wanted to help people believe that He had the power to forgive sins, which would bring them close to God again.

'I will make this man well,' He said. 'Then you will see that I also have the power to forgive the wrong things he has done.'

With that, Jesus said to the sick man kindly, 'Up you get. Pack up your bed and get off home.'

So the man did! He wasn't ill any more and his legs were better.

And that man sang songs of praise to God all the way home.

Because the sick man and his friends had faith, Jesus could make him well.

Can you sing a song to praise God right now?

Pens Prayer

Lord Jesus, You do such HUGE things. Help my faith to grow stronger as I live with You day by day. Amen

'Let us praise God for his glorious grace ...'
(Ephesians 1 v 6)

Different Pens

Why does Max always want to play football? It's so boring.

Max loves football.

'Why does Gloria always have to wear a hat?' frowned Denzil. 'It's so silly.'

Philippa replied, 'Gloria loves her hats.'

'Why does Charlotte always have to sing?' groaned Denzil. 'It's so annoying.'

Philippa replied, 'Charlotte loves to sing. Besides,' she added, 'we all enjoy different things. It's important to try to love our friends *because* of their differences – not complain about them.'

 Showing grace to others means loving and accepting them, not judging them and being unkind.

Think of one of your friends. Do you both like the same things? Or do you like different things?

Pens Prayer

You made each one of us to be different, Father God. Please help us to enjoy each other's differences, just as You do. Amen.

35

Day 17 — God of Grace

'My grace is all you need …' (2 Corinthians 12 v 9)

Splodge's Spill

Splodge was hiding. She'd spilt blackcurrant on Squiggle's favourite cushion and it wouldn't come off.

Squiggle's going to be so cross when she gets home.

The front door opened.

'I'm back, Splodge!' Squiggle called. 'Where are you?'

Splodge knew she couldn't hide forever.

'I'm here,' she said. 'And I'm so sorry about your cushion.'

Squiggle saw the purple marks. She frowned.

Then, 'Never mind,' she smiled. 'I'm sure we can wash them out.'

Splodge could hardly believe her ears. She was forgiven. Squiggle wasn't angry after all!

 God shows grace by forgiving us when we tell Him we are sorry.

If you accidentally spoil something that belongs to someone else, what is it always best to do?

Pens Prayer

Father God, please teach me how to forgive other people the way You forgive me. Amen.

Day 18 — God of Grace

'… continue to grow in the grace and knowledge of our Lord and Saviour Jesus Christ.' (2 Peter 3 v 18)

Who's going to the party?

Philippa decided to have a party.

She made a list of party food to get ready.

She made a list of party games to play.

She even made a list of party clothes she might wear.

Then, she made a list of all the friends she wanted to invite.

Marco read the names.

'Why are you inviting Gloria?' he asked. 'Gloria didn't invite you to her fancy hat party.'

'I know,' replied Philippa, 'but I can't leave her out. She's still one of my friends after all.'

 God likes us to be kind and forgiving to people all the time, not just because they've been kind to us.

Have you ever had a party? What kind of things did you do?

Pens Prayer

Dear Lord, thank You so much that You are always kind and loving towards me. I want to grow more like You every day. Amen.

There was mud in the kitchen.
Where could it have come from?

There was mud in the hallway.
Who could have put it there?

There was mud on the stairs.
How could that have happened?

There was mud on Max's bed.
What could be going on?

Mud wasn't the only thing on
Max's bed.

'Sharpy!' moaned Max.

Sharpy was fast asleep on Max's
pillow – and the mud from his paws
was everywhere.

But Sharpy looked so comfortable,
Max couldn't be cross.

'Come on,' he said kindly. 'I think it's
time for some paw-washing, don't you?'

God shows us grace by always
being patient with us when we
make mistakes.

What's the best
thing to wear if
you're going to play
where it's muddy?

Pens Prayer

Dear Lord, we all make mistakes
sometimes. Please help me to be
kind and understanding towards
my friends if they get something
wrong. Amen.

41

Day 20   God of Grace

'Show your love by being tolerant with one another.'
(Ephesians 4 v 2)

What Gloria wants

Charlotte was singing when she saw Gloria.

Shall we go for a walk?

No. I want to go shopping.

Marco was skateboarding when he saw Gloria. 'Shall we go to the park?' he grinned.

'No,' replied Gloria. 'I want to sit in my garden.'

Max was out with Sharpy when he saw Gloria. 'Come with us for a picnic,' he invited.

'No,' sighed Gloria. 'I want to read my book.'

'Gloria nearly always wants her own way,' frowned Marco.

'I know,' said Charlotte, 'but don't be cross. We can all be selfish sometimes.'

 Because of God's grace, He knows all our weaknesses but loves us anyway.

What is your favourite way to spend a day?

Pens Prayer

I'm sorry, Lord God, that sometimes I do and say things that make You sad. But thank You so much that whatever I do You still always love me. Amen.

43

God of Grace

'... God's mercy is so abundant, and his love for us is so great ...' (Ephesians 2 v 4)

The **missing** skateboard

'Where's my skateboard?' growled Denzil crossly. He'd looked everywhere.

In his room. Under the stairs. In the shed. He'd even looked behind the sofa. It was nowhere to be found.

Just then, Marco whizzed past – on Denzil's missing skateboard.

'Marco!' Denzil shouted. 'That's mine. Please give it back!'

Marco looked worried. 'Oh dear,' he mumbled. 'I didn't think you'd mind.'

Denzil could see Marco was sorry. 'I don't mind you using it,' he smiled. 'But next time you want to borrow something, please make sure you ask first.'

 God shows grace by forgiving us when we're sorry, instead of being cross with us.

Do you ever share your toys with others?

Pens Prayer

Please, Lord God, help me to be like You – and teach me to love and forgive my friends. Amen.

Day 22 God of Grace

'... by God's grace I am what I am ...'
(1 Corinthians 15 v 10)

The swimming lesson

Pens were at the pool. Splodge was learning to swim, but it was hard.

'Splodge splashes too much,' Max said. 'She'll never learn to swim like that.'

'Don't be unkind, Max,' replied Charlotte. 'Everyone has to start somewhere.'

'But swimming is so easy,' Max said smugly.

Charlotte shook her head. 'Just because you can swim doesn't mean you should look down on Splodge because she can't.' Then …

'Come on, Splodge!' Charlotte cheered. 'You can do it!'

 We show grace when we accept each other's differences and encourage one another – just as God does.

Is there anything new you'd like to learn to do?

Pens Prayer

Thank You, Father God, for the fun and excitement of learning to do new things. Amen.

'How great is the grace of God, which he gave to us in such large measure!' (Ephesians 1 vv 7–8)

Gloria's grumbles

Gloria was in a bad mood. Everything was wrong.

The sun was shining. But … 'It's too hot,' she moaned.

She bought a new hat. But … 'It's not comfy,' she grumbled.

She baked herself a cake. But … 'I'm not hungry,' she huffed.

Philippa asked, 'Can I help cheer you up?'

Gloria snapped, 'I don't want cheering up. Please go away.'

But Philippa picked a big bunch of flowers from her garden and gave them to Gloria anyway.

'Just for you,' Philippa smiled. 'Everyone needs cheering up sometimes.'

 God is kind to us even though we may not deserve it – which is how He shows 'grace'.

If you feel grumpy, how can you try to cheer yourself up?

Pens Prayer

Thank You, Lord God, that even when I feel grumpy, I can be sure of Your love. Amen.

49

Day 24 — God of Grace

'It is by God's grace that you have been saved.'
(Ephesians 2 v 5)

Naughty Sharpy

Max took Sharpy to the park.

But Sharpy spotted ducks on the pond.

'No!' shouted Max. Too late. Sharpy jumped into the water and swam after them.

Sharpy saw a cat snoozing on the grass.

'No!' shouted Max. Too late. Sharpy chased the cat up a tree.

Sharpy saw a picnic spread out on the ground.

'No!' shouted Max. Too late. Sharpy snatched a sandwich and ate it all up.

When they got home, Sharpy looked sorry.

'You've been very naughty,' Max scolded. 'I do love you, but please try to be good.'

God shows grace to us every day. He always loves us – in spite of the wrong things we do.

How can you show 'grace' to your friends?

Pens Prayer

Lord, I really thank You for loving me. Please help me to share Your love and grace with other people I know. Amen.

JONAH'S JOURNEY
Enough grace for everyone

Day 25

'Go to Nineveh, that great city, and speak out against it; I am aware how wicked its people are.' (Jonah 1 v 2)

'I won't!' says Jonah

God told Jonah to go to a place called Nineveh and tell the people who lived there to stop doing really bad things. God wanted them to change their ways so that He could forgive them.

This made Jonah grumpy.

'Those people are really very bad,' he thought. 'Why should they have the chance to be friends with God?'

So Jonah ran away. He sailed off on a ship that took him a long way from Nineveh.

The people of Nineveh made God sad with the terrible things they did, but God still wanted to be their Friend.

Do you ever find it difficult to forgive someone who has upset you?

Pens Prayer

You are always with me, always loving me and always ready to forgive any wrong things I may do. Thank You so much, Lord. Amen.

Jonah's Journey
Enough grace for everyone

Day 26 — 'But the LORD sent a strong wind on the sea, and the storm was so violent that the ship was in danger of breaking up.' (Jonah 1 v 4)

54

God didn't want Jonah to run away. He wanted him to speak to the people of Nineveh. So He sent a huge, howling storm.

Jonah was asleep on the ship.

'Wake up!' shouted the ship's captain. 'Ask God to save us!'

Jonah shook his head. 'God's angry because I'm not doing what He says,' he cried. 'Throw me off your ship. Then you'll be safe.'

'We're so sorry, Lord God,' sobbed the sailors, and they heaved Jonah into the sea.

Jonah thought he could run away from God, but God still had a plan for him.

How does God speak to us?

Pens Prayer

Dear Lord, sometimes I may not want to do what You want me to do. Please help me to remember that You really love me and only want the best for me. Amen.

Jonah's Journey
Enough grace for everyone

Day 27

'At the LORD's command a large fish swallowed Jonah, and he was inside the fish for three days and nights.' (Jonah 1 v 17)

A fishy escape

The waves roared. Jonah thought he would drown!

Then, all at once, God made everything calm. The ship was safe.

Poor Jonah wasn't. He was sinking fast.

Suddenly, an ENORMOUS fish swam up and swallowed him with one big gulp! It was dark in its tummy and there was a nasty smell. But Jonah knew God had sent the fish to save him.

'I'm sorry for running away, Lord,' he said. 'I'm ready to do as you say.'

Jonah said no to God, but God wanted to give him another chance to do what was right.

What do you think it would be like inside a big fish's tummy?

Pens Prayer

Thank You, Father God, that when we make mistakes You wait patiently for us to try again. Amen.

Jonah's Journey
Enough grace for everyone

Day 28
'So Jonah obeyed the LORD and went to Nineveh …' (Jonah 3 v 3)

'Yes,' says Jonah

58

God told the fish to spit Jonah out onto a beach. As Jonah sat on the sand, he heard God speaking to him again.

'Off you go to Nineveh. Tell everyone there that they have forty days to change their wicked ways. If they don't,' God warned, 'I will destroy their city.'

This time, Jonah didn't run away. This time, he went to Nineveh there and then. This time, he told everyone what God had said.

Jonah had done the wrong thing, but God still saved him and wanted him to be His messenger.

What special things would you like to be able to do?

Pens Prayer

Father God, You are Lord of the whole, HUGE world, yet You have a special purpose for ME. Thank You so much! Amen.

Day 29

'The people of Nineveh believed God's message.'
(Jonah 3 v 5)

Jonah gets cross

Jonah wasn't sure whether anyone in Nineveh would listen to him. But when all the people – even the king – began to cry, 'We're sorry, Lord God. Please forgive us!' Jonah could hardly believe his ears.

'No!' he complained to God. 'Now you won't destroy these people. You'll forgive them instead because You are kind and loving. But they don't deserve Your forgiveness. They've been much too terrible! That's why I didn't want to tell them what You'd said.'

Jonah was grumpy all over again.

God wants to forgive people even when they don't deserve it.

How can you let God know that you love Him and want to make Him happy?

Pens Prayer

Heavenly Father, the way You care for me is amazing. Thank You. Amen.

Jonah's Journey
Enough grace for everyone

Day 30

'... you are a loving and merciful God, always patient, always kind, and always ready to change your mind and not punish.' (Jonah 4 v 2)

God's Grace

Jonah sat down grumpily to rest. God made a vine grow to shade him from the sun. It cheered Jonah up and he fell asleep.

But, in the night, God sent a wriggly worm and it killed the vine.

'What have You done?' Jonah grumbled.

God answered, 'Why do you care more about a vine than about my people in Nineveh? I love them and have forgiven them. You must forgive them, too.'

God forgave the people of Nineveh for their bad ways and He forgave Jonah for running away. God has enough love and grace for everyone.

How can you let your family and friends know about God's amazing love? Can you tell them this story?

Pens Prayer

Father God, thank You so much that even though You don't always like the things I do, You'll never stop loving me. Amen.

Other Pens titles

Visit www.cwr.org.uk/distributors for list of National Distributors.

All Scripture references are from the GNB: Good News Bible © American Bible Society 1966, 1971, 1976, 1992. Used with permission.

Concept development, editing, design and production by CWR.

Printed in China by 1010 Printing Ltd.

ISBN: 978-1-85345-570-4

OTHER CWR DAILY BIBLE-READING NOTES
Every Day with Jesus for adults
Inspiring Women Every Day for women
Lucas on Life Every Day for adults
Cover to Cover Every Day for adults
Mettle for 14- to 18-year-olds
YP's for 11- to 15-year-olds
Topz for 7- to 11-year-olds